CODE WITH CHEENAKSHI

CHEENAKSHI GUPTA

Contents

CHAPTER I

Introduction to Programming

Programming is the process of creating instructions that a computer can follow to perform specific tasks. It involves writing and designing code in a programming language to solve problems, automate tasks, or create software applications.

What is Programming?

Programming is like giving a computer a set of step-by-step instructions to complete a task. These instructions are written in a language that the computer understands, such as Python, Java, or JavaScript.

Why Learn Programming?

- **Solve Problems:** Automate repetitive tasks and solve real-world problems.
- **Career Opportunities:** Programming skills are in high demand across industries.
- **Creativity:** Build websites, games, apps, and more.
- **Critical Thinking:** Develop logical thinking and problem-solving skills.

Introduction of Programming Language

As we know, to communicate with a person, we need a specific language, similarly to communicate with computers, programmers also need a language is called Programming language.

The tools used by software engineers to write down computer packages are programming languages. They are the means of interacting with and commanding computer systems. Numerous distinct programming languages exist, each with its benefits and downsides. Certain languages are more appropriate for optimistic roles than others. For example, some languages are made for basic programming, while others are made for specific fields like networking, statistics generation, and web and app development.

What is a Programming Language?

A programming language is a computer language that is used by programmers (developers) to communicate with computers. It is a set of instructions written in any specific language (C, C++, Java, Python) to perform a specific task.

A programming language is mainly used to develop desktop applications, websites, and mobile applications.

What is the need for programming languages?

Several software packages are made using programming languages, together with:

- Operating structures
- Web browsers
- Mobile apps
- Desktop packages
- Video games
- General Software program
- Business-related software programs
- Embedded structures

Types of programming language

1. Low-level programming language

Low-level language is machine-dependent (0s and 1s) programming language. The processor runs low- level programs directly without the need of a compiler or interpreter, so the programs written in low-level language can be run very fast.

Low-level language is further divided into two parts -
i. Machine Language

Machine language is a type of low-level programming language. It is also called as machine code or object code. Machine language is easier to read because it is normally displayed in binary or hexadecimal form (base 16) form. It does not require a translator to convert the programs because computers directly understand the machine language programs.

The advantage of machine language is that it helps the programmer to execute the programs faster than the high-level programming language.

ii. Assembly Language

Assembly language (ASM) is also a type of low-level programming language that is designed for specific processors. It represents the set of instructions in a symbolic and human-understandable form. It uses an assembler to convert the assembly language to machine language.

The advantage of assembly language is that it requires less memory and less execution time to execute a program.

2. High-level programming language

High-level programming language (HLL) is designed for developing user-friendly software programs and websites. This programming language requires a compiler or interpreter to translate the program into machine language (execute the program).

The main advantage of a high-level language is that it is easy to read, write, and maintain.

High-level programming language includes Python, Java, JavaScript, PHP, C#, C++, Objective C, Cobol, Perl, Pascal, LISP, FORTRAN, and Swift programming language.

A high-level language is further divided into three parts -

i. Procedural Oriented programming language

Procedural Oriented Programming (POP) language is derived from structured programming and based upon the procedure call concept. It divides a program into small procedures called routines or functions.

Procedural Oriented programming language is used by a software programmer to create a program that can be accomplished by using a programming editor like IDE, Adobe Dreamweaver, or Microsoft Visual Studio.

The advantage of POP language is that it helps programmers to easily track the program flow and code can be reused in different parts of the program.

Example: C, FORTRAN, Basic, Pascal, etc.

ii. Object-Oriented Programming language

Object-Oriented Programming (OOP) language is based upon the objects. In this programming language, programs are divided into small parts called objects. It is used to implement real-world entities like inheritance, polymorphism, abstraction etc. in the program to makes the program reusable, efficient, and easy-to-use.

The main advantage of object-oriented programming is that OOP is faster and easier to execute, maintain, modify, as well as debug.

Example: C++, Java, Python, C#, etc.

iii. Natural language

Natural language is a part of human languages such as English, Russian, German, and Japanese. It is used by machines to understand, manipulate, and interpret human's language. It is used by developers to perform tasks such as translation, automatic summarization, Named Entity Recognition (NER), relationship extraction, and topic segmentation.

The main advantage of natural language is that it helps users to ask questions in any subject and directly respond within seconds.

3. Middle-level programming language

Middle-level programming language lies between the low-level programming language and high-level programming language. It is also known as the intermediate programming language and pseudo-language.

A middle-level programming language's advantages are that it supports the features of high-level programming, it is a user-friendly language, and closely related to machine language and human language.

Example: C, C++, language

Problem Solving Using Computers:

In order to develop a program, whether it is small or complex a special procedure to be followed which is called as program development life cycle . The problem is the systematic way of developing any quality software.

To solve a problem efficiently , the programmer follows the following steps referred to as the programming process:

- Problem definition and Analysis
- Program design
- Coding
- Compilation
- Debugging and Testing
- Documentation
- Implementation and Maintenance

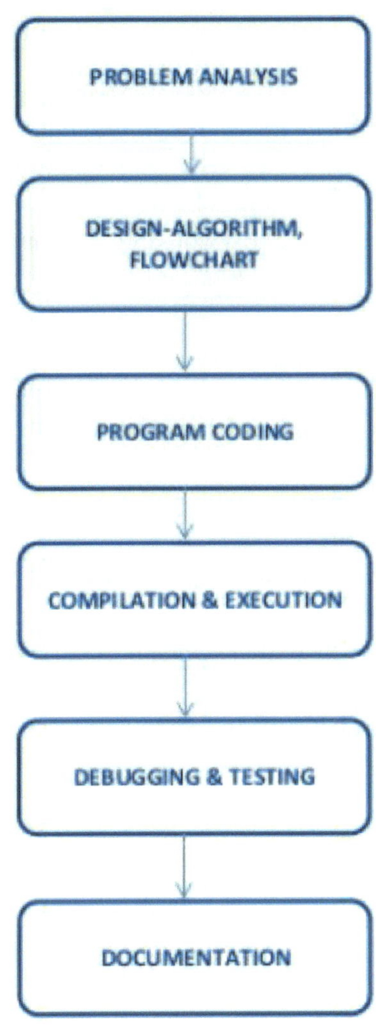

Problem Solving Process

1. Problem Definition and Analysis:

Explain the problem clearly as possible as you can. First, figure out what needs to be solved. Break the problem into smaller parts to make it easier to understand

What it means: Clearly understanding what the problem is and what the goal is.

Purpose: To ensure that you and the computer "know" exactly what needs to be done.

Steps:

- Identify the input: What data will the computer need?
- Identify the output: What result should the computer produce?
- Set clear boundaries: What the program should and should NOT do.

Example:
Problem: Calculate the average of 5 numbers.
Input: 5 numbers (e.g., 10, 20, 30, 40, 50).
Output: The average (e.g., 30).

Problem Analysis

What it means: Breaking the problem into smaller, manageable parts to figure out the steps required to solve it.

Purpose: To create a clear plan (algorithm) for solving the problem.

Key Questions to Ask:

1. What are the steps needed to solve the problem?

2. Are there any constraints (e.g., limits on input)?
3. What tools or methods will you use?

Example Analysis for Average Problem:
Step 1: Collect 5 numbers.
Step 2: Add the numbers together.
Step 3: Divide the total by 5.
Step 4: Display the result.

2. Program Design

List out all the solution that you find. Don't focus on the quality of the solution . Generate the maximum number of solution as you can without considering the quality of the solution decide how the computer should solve the problem.

Use a step-by-step plan (called an algorithm) to explain the process or explain with diagram(flowchart)

Algorithm:

Algorithm is the set of rules that define how particular problem can be solved in finite number of steps. Any good algorithm must have following characteristics

Input: Specify and require input

Output: Solution of any problem

Definite: Solution must be clearly defined

Finite: Steps must be finite

Correct: Correct output must be generated

Advantages of Algorithms:

- It is the way to resolve a problem step-wise so it is easy to understand.
- It uses definite procedure.
- It is not dependent with any programming language.

- Each step has its own meaning so it is easy to debug

Disadvantage of Algorithms:

- It is time consuming
- Difficult to show branching and looping statement
- Large problems are difficult to implement

Flowchart:

The solution of any problem in picture form is called flowchart. It is the one of the most important technique to depict an algorithm.

Advantage of Flowchart:

- Easier to understand
- Helps to understand logic of problem
- Easy to draw flowchart in any software like MS-Word
- Complex problem can be represent using less symbols
- It is the way to documenting any problem
- Helps in debugging process

Disadvantage of Flowchart:

- For any change, Flowchart have to redrawn
- Showing many looping and branching become complex
- Modification of flowchart is time consuming

Example
Algorithm:
Step 1: Start
Step 2: Declare a variable x
Step 3: Take a input from user and store in x
Step 4: IF x % 2 == 0 THEN

PRINT Even
ELSE
PRINT Odd
Step 5: End

Flowchart Symbols

Symbol	Name	Function
	Start/end	An oval represents a start or end point
	Arrows	A line is a connector that shows relationships between the representative shapes
	Input/Output	A parallelogram represents input or output
	Process	A rectangle represents a process
	Decision	A diamond indicates a decision

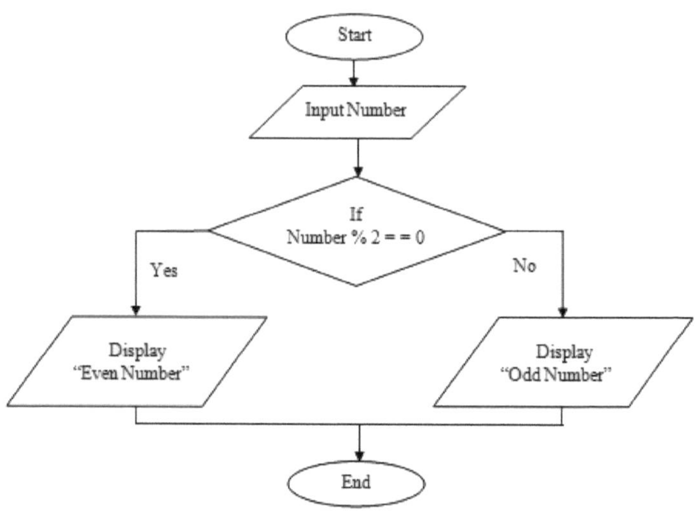

3. Coding

Transform your algorithm into code using a programming language.

Focus on:

Syntax: Ensure the code is syntactically correct.

Logic: Make sure the implementation matches the intended algorithm.

4. Compilation

It refers to the process of converting source code written in a high-level programming language into machine code (binary format) so that the computer can execute it. It is a crucial step in solving problems using programming, as it ensures the written code is syntactically and logically correct before execution.

Steps of Compilation in Problem Solving

Write Code:

The problem-solving process begins with writing a program in a high-level language (e.g., C, C++, Java, Python).

Example: Writing an algorithm to sort an array.

Compilation Process:

Preprocessing:

Handles preprocessor directives (e.g., #include, #define in C/C++).

Removes comments and expands macros.

Lexical Analysis:

Converts the code into tokens (basic language elements like keywords, identifiers, etc.).

Syntax Analysis:

Checks for syntax errors in the code (e.g., missing semicolons or mismatched brackets).

Semantic Analysis:

Ensures the code is logically valid (e.g., checking data types, proper variable usage).

Intermediate Code Generation:

Converts the source code into an intermediate representation (e.g., abstract syntax trees).

Optimization:

Improves the code for better performance (reduces redundant calculations, minimizes memory usage).

Code Generation:

Produces machine code or bytecode.

Linking:

Combines compiled code with libraries or other program modules into an executable.

Advantages of Compilation in Problem Solving

Error Detection:

Compilation identifies syntax and semantic errors before running the program.

Example: Using a variable without declaring it will result in a compilation error.

Performance:

Compiled programs run faster as they are converted to machine code before execution.

Portability:

Compilers for high-level languages like C/C++ allow the same source code to be compiled for different platforms.

Optimization:

Modern compilers optimize code for speed and memory, which is critical for solving complex problems efficiently.

Execution:

The compiled code is executed, producing the solution to the problem.

5. Debugging and Testing

Debugging

If the solution doesn't work as expected, debugging is done to fix errors detected during compilation (syntax, semantic, or logical).

Testing

Testing ensures your code works for all inputs, not just one. Testing in problem-solving with computers means checking if the solution (program or algorithm) works correctly. It involves running the program with different inputs to see if it gives the right outputs. If there are errors or unexpected results, you fix them. This helps ensure the solution is accurate and reliable.

Debugging vs. Testing

- Aspect
- Debugging
- Testing
- Purpose
- Find and fix errors in your code.
- Verify the program works correctly.
- When?
- During development.
- After writing or fixing the code.
- How?
- Use tools like print or debuggers.
- Use test cases (manual or automated)

Tips for Effective Debugging and Testing

Start with simple test cases, then move to complex ones.

Write modular code (small functions) to make debugging easier.

Test after every small change to the code.

Look for patterns in errors to fix recurring issues.

6. Documentation

It means writing clear, detailed explanations about your code, algorithms, or approach so others (or even your future self!) can understand it easily. It's an essential part of programming because it helps in understanding, using, and maintaining your solution.

Why is Documentation Important?

Clarity: Explains what the code does and why.

Collaboration: Helps teammates understand your code.

Debugging & Maintenance: Makes fixing or updating code easier.

Learning: Others (and you) can learn from your approach.

7. Implementation

Implementation means putting the solution (like a program) into action. Once the program is written and tested, it is installed and made ready for actual use. This step ensures that the program is working as intended in the real environment where users can interact with it.

Important Points for Better Implementation

Write Step by Step: Don't try to do everything at once.

Start Simple: Begin with a basic version, then improve it.

Test Often: Test your code after each small part is done.

Use Built-In Functions: Use helpful features of the programming language.

8. *Maintenance*

It means improving, fixing, or updating your code after it's already written and working. It ensures the solution stays correct, efficient, and useful over time. Maintenance is important because real-world problems often change, and software needs to adapt.

Maintenance means keeping the solution working properly over time. After implementation, problems may appear, or updates may be needed due to changes in requirements

Why is Maintenance Important?

Fix Bugs: Errors might be discovered after the code is used.

Handle Changes: New features or requirements may be added.

Optimize Performance: Make the code faster or use less memory.

Ensure Compatibility: Update the code to work with newer technologies or systems.

Advantages of Maintenance

Keeps the program running smoothly.

Adapts the solution to new needs.

Saves time in the future by preventing bigger problems.

CHAPTER II

Basic of C Programming

Introduction to C Language

C is a procedural programming language initially developed by Dennis Ritchie in the year 1972 at Bell Laboratories of AT&T Labs. It was mainly developed as a system programming language to write the UNIX operating system. C was designed for system programming (like operating systems) but is also used for creating applications, games, and embedded systems.

Why Learn C?

It builds a strong foundation for learning other languages.

C is still widely used in areas like embedded systems, game development, and operating systems.

It helps understand how computers work at a deeper level.

History of c

The C programming language has a fascinating history that dates back to the late 1960s and early 1970s. Here's a concise timeline of its development:

1. Origins and Early Development (1960s)

C evolved from earlier programming languages like B, BCPL (Basic Combined Programming Language), and ALGOL 60.

BCPL (developed by Martin Richards in 1966) and B (developed by Ken Thompson in 1969) were influential predecessors of C.

2. Birth of C at Bell Labs (1972)

Dennis Ritchie developed C at Bell Laboratories while working on the UNIX operating system.

C was created to overcome the limitations of B and to provide a more powerful, flexible, and portable language for system programming.

C's design allowed close interaction with hardware while retaining high-level functionality.

3. C and UNIX (1970s)

C played a pivotal role in rewriting the UNIX operating system, making it portable and platform-independent.

The combination of UNIX and C became popular and influential in the computing world.

4. Standardization and Spread (1980s)

By the 1980s, C gained immense popularity for both system and application programming.

In 1983, ANSI (American National Standards Institute) began standardizing C, leading to the release of ANSI C (C89) in 1989.

This version became the widely adopted standard and introduced features like function prototypes, standard libraries, and better type checking.

5. Modern Updates

C99 (1999): Introduced new features like inline functions, variable-length arrays, and better floating-point support.

C11 (2011): Brought features such as multithreading, anonymous structures, and improved Unicode support.

C17 (2017): Focused on minor refinements and bug fixes.

C23 (2023): Included further improvements, enhancing usability and modern programming requirements.

6. Legacy

C is considered one of the most influential programming languages. It served as the foundation for many modern languages like C++, Java, Python, and C#. It remains widely used for system-level programming, embedded systems, and performance-critical applications.

Features of the C language

1. Simple and Easy to Learn

C has a straightforward syntax with basic commands, making it easy to understand and learn.

2. Structured Language

C allows you to break a program into smaller parts (called functions) for better organization and readability.

3. Portable

C programs can run on different machines with minimal changes, making it a portable language.

4. Fast and Efficient

C is close to the hardware (low-level), so it runs programs quickly and uses resources efficiently.

5. Rich Library

It provides a variety of built-in functions for tasks like input/output, string handling, math operations, etc.

6. Supports Low-Level Programming

You can directly work with hardware and memory (using pointers), which is essential for system programming.

7. Extensible

You can create and use your own functions in addition to the built-in ones, which makes it customizable.

8. Statically Typed

C requires you to define the type of variables (e.g., int, float) before using them, helping avoid errors.

9. Supports Pointers

C allows direct memory management using pointers, which is a powerful feature for system-level programming.

10. Versatile

C is used for a wide range of applications, from operating systems (like UNIX) to embedded systems and game development.

Applications

C is a versatile and powerful language used in many domains. Here are some major applications of the C language:

1. Operating Systems

C is used to develop operating systems like UNIX, Linux, Windows, and macOS.

Its low-level features and speed make it perfect for OS development.

2. Embedded Systems

C is widely used in microcontrollers and embedded devices like washing machines, microwaves, and automotive systems.

Its ability to interact directly with hardware makes it ideal for these applications.

3. System Software

C is used to create compilers, interpreters, device drivers, and system utilities.

4. Game Development

Game engines and high-performance gaming applications often use C due to its efficiency.

Example: The Quake game engine was developed using C.

5. Databases

Popular databases like MySQL, Oracle Database, and SQLite are developed in C.

C's performance and memory management make it suitable for database systems

6. Graphics and Animation

C is used in graphics applications like OpenGL for rendering images, simulations, and animations.

7. Network Programming

Many network tools and protocols (e.g., FTP, HTTP) are built using C.

It is used in socket programming to create servers and clients.

8. Scientific and Engineering Applications

C is used in mathematical computations, simulations, and modeling tools.

9. Desktop Applications

Many software applications like text editors and media players are built using C.

Example: Notepad and VLC Media Player use components written in C.

10. IoT (Internet of Things)

C plays a key role in IoT devices, where small-scale hardware needs lightweight and efficient programming.

Structure of the C Program

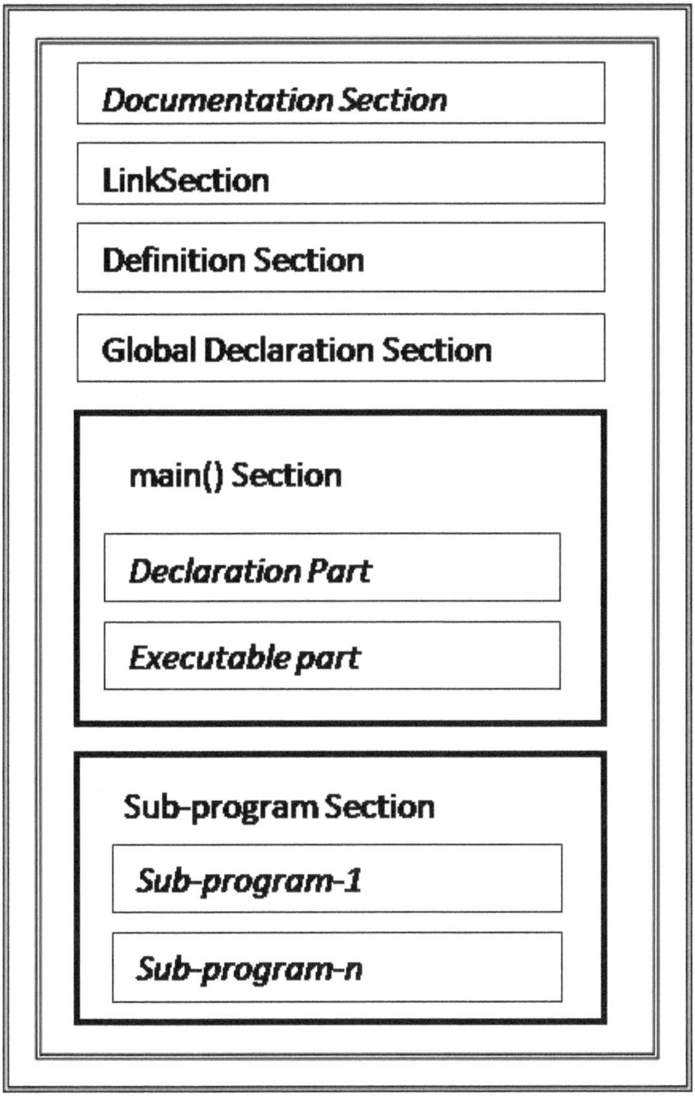

Documentation Section

LinkSection

Definition Section

Global Declaration Section

main() Section

Declaration Part

Executable part

Sub-program Section

Sub-program-1

Sub-program-n

Structure of the C Program

Documentation Section:

This section contains information about the program such as author name, creation data & time etc. It provides guidelines to the program reader. It may also include logic of the program. This information is written as a comment.

It is represented as:

//name of a program

Or

/*

Overview of the code

.

*/

Both methods work as the document section in a program. It provides an overview of the program. Anything written inside will be considered a part of the documentation section and will not interfere with the specified code.

Link Section:

It includes different library and header files that are required by the program. These header files are linked with the program during the linking steps. Some standard header files are <stdio.h>,<conio.h>, <string.h> etc.

The preprocessor section contains all the header files used in a program. It informs the system to link the header files to the system libraries. It is given by:

#include<stdio.h>

#include<conio.h>

The #include statement includes the specific file as a part of a function at the time of the compilation. Thus, the contents of the included file are compiled along with the function being compiled. The #include<stdio.h> consists of the contents of the standard input output files, which contains the definition of stdin, stdout, and stderr.

Whenever the definitions stdin, stdout, and stderr are used in a function, the statement #include<stdio.h> need to be used. There are various header files available for different purposes. For example, # include <math.h>. It is used for mathematic functions in a program.

Definition Section:

This section includes all the constant variables. They are defined with the "#define"

Global Declaration Section:

All the global variables are defined in this section. Global variables can be accessed by any function of the program. Their scope is entire program.

main () Section:

The main () section is the main section of the C-program. Each C- program must have one and only one main function. It is define using main ()

Every statement of the C- program should be written in the main section.

Opening '{'specifies starting of the main function and closing '}' specifies ending of the main function. main section is divided into the following two sections.

Declaration part Executable part

Declaration part contains all the local variables to be used in the main section.

Executable section contains all the executable statement to perform the task.

Sub-program Section:

This section includes all the sub-program definitions. It is used when program is divided into different functions. Its order is not important; it can be place before or after the main section. Normlly it is written after the main section..

Example: --To find the sum of two numbers given by the user

```c
/* Sum of two numbers */
#include<stdio.h>
int main()
{
int a, b, sum;
printf ("Enter two numbers to be added ");
scanf ("%d %d", &a, &b);
// calculating sum
sum = a + b;
printf ("%d + %d = %d", a, b, sum);
return 0; // return the integer value in the sum
}
```

Output

The detailed explanation of each part of a code is as follows:

/* Sum of the two numbers */

It is the comment section. Any statement described in it is not considered as a code. It is a part of the description section in a code.

The comment line is optional. It can be in a separate line or part of an executable line.

#include<stdio.h>

It is the standard input-output header file. It is a command of the preprocessor section.

int main ()

main () is the first function to be executed in every program. We have used int with the main () in order to return an integer value.

{...
}

The curly braces mark the beginning and end of a function. It is mandatory in all the functions.

printf ()

The printf () prints text on the screen. It is a function for displaying constant or variables data. Here, 'Enter two numbers to be added' is the parameter passed to it.

scanf ()

It reads data from the standard input stream and writes the result into the specified arguments.

sum = a + b

The addition of the specified two numbers will be passed to the sum parameter in the output.

return 0

A program can also run without a return 0 function. It simply states that a program is free from error and can be successfully exited.

Summary:

Preprocessor directives: Start with #.

Global declarations: For shared variables.

Main function: Entry point of the program.

Local variables: Declared inside functions.

Executable code: Includes statements and expressions.

User-defined functions/sub-program: For reusability and clarity.

Errors in C language

1. Syntax Errors or Compiler Errors

When it occurs: During compilation.

What it is: Mistakes in using the C programming language syntax rules.

Examples:

Missing semicolons (;).

Using undeclared variables.

Incorrect function calls.

2. Semantic Errors

When it occurs: During compilation or runtime.

What it is: Errors in the logic or meaning of the code that make it behave incorrectly.

Examples:

Assigning incompatible types.

Using operations in an invalid context.

3. Runtime Errors

When it occurs: While the program is running.

What it is: Errors that occur during the program's execution, typically due to invalid operations.

Examples:

Division by zero.

Accessing invalid memory.

4. Logical Errors

When it occurs: The program runs, but the output is incorrect.

What it is: Errors in the algorithm or logic used in the program.

Examples:

Incorrect conditions in if statements.

Misuse of operators.

5. Linker Errors

When it occurs: During the linking phase of the compilation process.

What it is: Errors due to missing definitions, multiple definitions, or unresolved external references.

Examples:

Missing library functions.

Undefined functions.

CHAPTER III

Constants,Variables and Data Types

Introduction

Constants

A constant is a value that cannot be changed while the program is running. : Fixed values that don't change.

Example: Numbers like 10, characters like 'A', or fixed values like 3.14 are constants.

In C, you can use the const keyword to define constants.
const int age = 25; // The value of age cannot change.

Variables

A variable is like a container used to store data that can change during the program's execution.

You give a variable a name, a type, and then assign it a value.

int number = 10; // 'number' is a variable of type integer.

Data Types

Data types define the kind of data a variable can store. Define the type of data a variable can hold. Containers to store changeable data.

Common data types in C:

int: Stores whole numbers (e.g., 10, -5).
float: Stores decimal numbers (e.g., 3.14, -2.5).
char: Stores single characters (e.g., 'A', 'Z').
double: Stores larger decimal numbers (e.g., 3.141592).

Character set

C is a collection of characters that can be used in a C program to form words, numbers, and expressions. It includes uppercase and lowercase letters, digits, special symbols, and white space characters.

Letters: The uppercase and lowercase English alphabet (A-Z and a-z)

Digits: The numbers 0–9

Special characters: Symbols for mathematical operations, logical operations, punctuation, and more

Whitespace characters: Spaces, tabs, newlines, and form feeds

Escape sequences: Special meaning characters that start with a backslash, such as \n (newline), \t (tab), and \' (single quote)

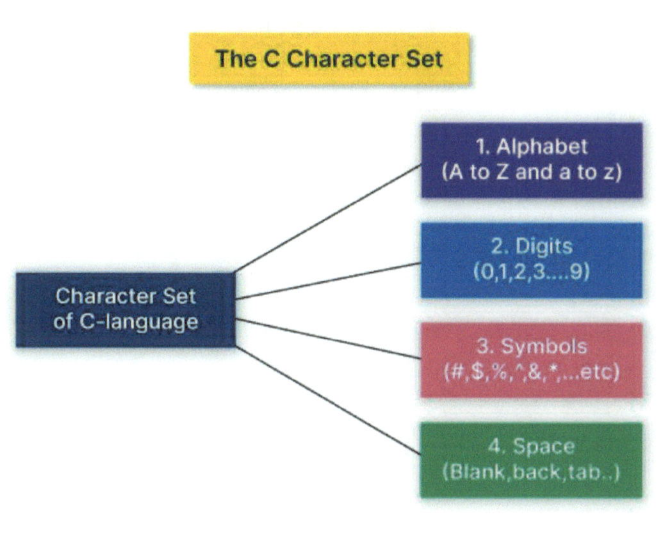

The C Character Set

Tokens

Tokens in C is the most important element to be used in creating a program in C. We can define the token as the smallest individual element in C. For `example, we cannot create a sentence without using words; similarly, we cannot create a program in C without using tokens in C. Hence tokens are the smallest building blocks of a program. Everything in a C program is made up of tokens.

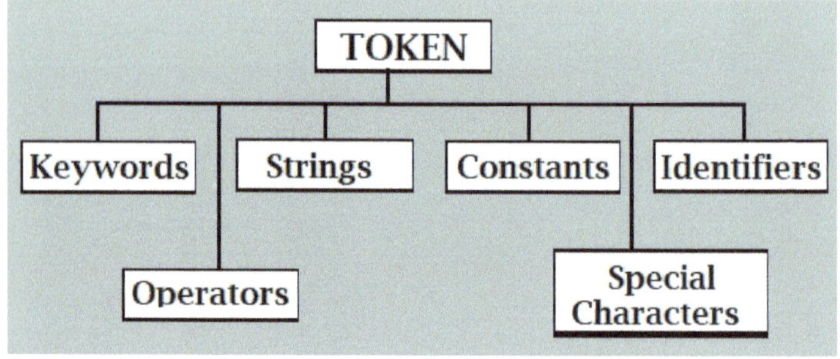

Tokens

- Keywords
- Identifiers
- Strings
- Operators
- Constant
- Special Characters

Keywords

It can be defined as the pre-defined or the reserved words having its own importance, and each keyword has its own functionality. Since keywords are the pre-defined words used by the compiler, so they cannot be used as the variable names. keywords are always written in lowercase. If the keywords are used as the variable names, it means that we are assigning a different meaning to the keyword, which is not allowed. C language supports 32 keywords given below:

- auto

- double
- int
- struct
- break
- else
- long
- switch
- case
- enum
- register
- typedef
- char
- extern
- return
- union
- const
- float
- short
- unsigned
- continue
- for
- signed
- void
- default
- goto
- sizeof
- volatile
- do
- If
- static
- while

Identifiers

Identifiers are used for naming variables, functions, arrays, structures, etc. Identifiers in C are the user-defined words. It can be composed of uppercase letters, lowercase letters, underscore, or digits, but the starting letter should be either an underscore or an alphabet. Identifiers cannot be used as keywords. Rules for constructing identifiers in C are given below:

The first character of an identifier should be either an alphabet or an underscore, and then it can be followed by any of the character, digit, or underscore.

It should not begin with any numerical digit.

- In identifiers, both uppercase and lowercase letters are distinct. Therefore, we can say that identifiers are case sensitive.
- Commas or blank spaces cannot be specified within an identifier.
- Keywords cannot be represented as an identifier.
- The length of the identifiers should not be more than 31 characters.
- Identifiers should be written in such a way that it is meaningful, short, and easy to read.

Strings

Strings are always represented as an array of characters having null character '\0' at the end of the string. This null character denotes the end of the string. Strings in C are enclosed within double quotes, while characters are enclosed within single characters. The size of a string is a number of characters that the string contains.

Operators

Operator is a special symbol used to perform the functions. The data items on which the operators are applied are known as operands. Operators are applied between the operands. Depending on the number of operands, operators are classified as follows:

Unary Operator

A unary operator is an operator applied to the single operand. For example: increment operator (++), decrement operator (--), sizeof, (type).

Binary Operator

The binary operator is an operator applied between two operands. The following is the list of the binary operators:

- Arithmetic Operators
- Relational Operators
- Shift Operators
- Logical Operators
- Bitwise Operators
- Conditional Operators
- Assignment Operator
- Misc Operator
- Constants

A constant is a value assigned to the variable which will remain the same throughout the program, i.e., the constant value cannot be changed.

There are two ways of declaring constant:

Using const keyword

Using #define pre-processor

Syntax: const data_type var_name = value;

Types of constants in C

Integer constant

10, 11, 34, etc.

Floating-point constant

45.6, 67.8, 11.2, etc.

Octal constant

011, 088, 022, etc.

Hexadecimal constant

0x1a, 0x4b, 0x6b, etc.

Character constant

'a', 'b', 'c', etc.

String constant

"java", "c++", ".net", etc.

Special characters in C

Some special characters are used in C, and they have a special meaning which cannot be used for another purpose.

Square brackets [ ]: The opening and closing brackets represent the single and multidimensional subscripts.

Simple brackets ( ): It is used in function declaration and function calling. For example, printf() is a pre-defined function.

Curly braces { }: It is used in the opening and closing of the code. It is used in the opening and closing of the loops.

Comma (,): It is used for separating for more than one statement and for example, separating function parameters in a function call, separating the variable when printing the value of more than one variable using a single printf statement.

Hash/pre-processor (#): It is used for pre-processor directive. It basically denotes that we are using the header file.

Asterisk (*): This symbol is used to represent pointers and also used as an operator for multiplication.

Tilde (~): It is used as a destructor to free memory.

Period (.): It is used to access a member of a structure or a union.

Variables

variables are names given to memory locations that store data values. These variables allow you to manipulate and retrieve data during program execution. Here's an overview:

Declaration and Initialization

Declaration: Specifies the type of data a variable can hold.

int number; // Declaration of an integer variable

Initialization: Assigns a value to the variable.

int number = 10; // Initialization

Syntax of Variable Declaration

data_type variable_name;

data_type: Determines the type of data the variable can hold (e.g., int, float, char).

variable_name: Follows naming rules and represents the variable.

Types of Variables

(a) Local Variables

Declared inside a function or block.

Accessible only within the scope of the function or block.

```
void example ()
{
int a = 5; // Local variable
}
```

(b) Global Variables

Declared outside all functions.

Accessible to all functions in the program.

```
int b = 20; // Global variable
void example ()
{
printf ("%d", b);
}
```

(c) Static Variables

Retain their value across multiple function calls.

Default value is zero.

```
void example ()
{
static int c = 0; // Static variable
c++;
printf ("%d", c);
}
```

(d) External Variables

Declared using the extern keyword, indicating the variable is defined elsewhere.

Syntax extern int e;

(e) Register Variables

Stored in CPU registers for faster access (if possible).

Declared using the register keyword.

Syntax register int counter;

Variable Naming Rules

Must start with a letter or an underscore (_).

Cannot use reserved keywords (e.g., int, while).

No special characters (e.g., @, $) except _.

Case-sensitive (var and Var are different).

Data Types

In C language, data types define the type of data a variable can hold. These data types are broadly categorized into the following:

Primary Data Types or Predefined Data Type or In built Data Types

Int:-> int data type is used to represent integer numbers. These are whole numbers (both positive and negative) without any fractional or decimal part.

Key Features of int:

Size:

The size of an int depends on the system or compiler, but it is typically 4 bytes (32 bits) on modern systems.

It can store values in the range of:

Signed int: -2,147,483,648 to 2,147,483,647 (when 4 bytes are used)

Unsigned int: 0 to 4,294,967,295

Usage:

It is declared using the keyword int.

For example:

int age = 25; // Declares a variable named 'age' with value 25

Signed and Unsigned Variants:

By default, int is signed, meaning it can hold both positive and negative numbers.

Use unsigned int if you want to store only non-negative values.

signed int x = -10; // Explicitly signed (default)

unsigned int y = 100; // Unsigned integer

Example:

#include <stdio.h>

int main ()

{

int a = 10; // signed integer

unsigned int b = 20; // unsigned integer

printf ("Value of a: %d\n", a);

printf ("Value of b: %u\n", b);

return 0;

}

Format Specifiers:

Use %d or %i for signed integers.

Use %u for unsigned integers in printf.

float data type:- It is used to store floating-point numbers, which are numbers with decimal points or fractions. It is ideal for representing real numbers where precision is required for fractional values.

Key Features of float:

Size and Precision:

Typically, a float occupies 4 bytes (32 bits) in memory.

It provides approximately 6 to 7 decimal digits of precision.

Example: 3.141592 is an approximate value of π.

Range:

The range of values for float is from approximately:

$\pm 1.5 \times 10^{-45}$ to $\pm 3.4 \times 10^{38}$

This range makes it suitable for scientific computations with a moderate level of precision.

Usage:

It is declared using the keyword float. For example:

float pi = 3.14;

Example :

```
#include <stdio.h>
int main () {
float number1 = 3.14; // Assigning a floating-point value
float number2 = -5.678; // Negative floating-point value
printf ("Number 1: %.2f\n", number1); // Output with 2 decimal places
printf ("Number 2: %.3f\n", number2); // Output with 3 decimal places
return 0;
}
```

Output:

Number 1: 3.14

Number 2: -5.678

Format Specifier:

Use %f to print floating-point numbers.

You can control the number of decimal places using %.nf, where n is the number of decimal places.

Mathematical Operations:

You can perform addition, subtraction, multiplication, and division with floating-point numbers.

float a = 5.5, b = 2.2;

float result = a + b; // Addition

printf ("Result: %.1f\n", result); // Output: 7.7

char:-It is used to store a single character. It is one of the most basic and commonly used data types in C, primarily for working with characters and strings.

Key Features of char:

Size:

A char occupies 1 byte (8 bits) in memory.

It can represent 256 different values (2^8), ranging from -128 to 127 for signed char, or 0 to 255 for unsigned char.

Usage:

The char data type is used to store a single character (e.g., 'A', 'z', '3', etc.).

Characters are enclosed in single quotes (').

char letter = 'A'; // Stores the character 'A'

Format Specifier:

Use %c to print a character in printf.

Example:

char ch = 'Z';

printf ("Character: %c\n", ch);

String Representation:

Strings in C are arrays of characters terminated by a null character (\0).

Example:

char str[] = "Hello"; // Array of characters

printf ("%s", str); // Output: Hello

Signed and Unsigned char:

By default, char is signed in most compilers, meaning it can hold negative values.

To ensure only non-negative values (0 to 255), use unsigned char.

Example :

```
#include <stdio.h>
int main ()
{
char letter = 'A'; // A single character
char symbol = '$'; // A special character
char digit = '5'; // Digit as a character
printf ("Letter: %c\n", letter);
printf ("Symbol: %c\n", symbol);
printf ("Digit: %c (ASCII: %d) \n", digit, digit); // ASCII
value of '5' is 53
return 0;
}
```

Output:

Letter: A

Symbol: $

Digit: 5 (ASCII: 53)

User-defined data types: The data types defined by the user themself are referred to as user-defined data types.

struct (Structure):

A structure is a collection of variables (of different or the same types) grouped together under a single name.

Example:

```
struct Student {
char name [50];
int age;
float marks;
};
```

union:

A union is similar to a structure but shares memory among its members, so only one member can hold a value at a time.

Example:

union Data {

int i;

float f;

char str [20];

};

enum (Enumeration):

Enumerations are used to define a set of named integer constants, improving code readability.

Example:

enum Color { RED , GREEN, BLUE };

typedef:

Used to create an alias for an existing data type, making code easier to read.

Example:

typedef unsigned int uint;

uint age = 25;

Derived Data Type:-> In C, derived data types are types that are created from the basic data types (like int, float, char) through some modifications or combinations. These are used to store collections or more complex forms of data. Derived from the primary types

Array:

A collection of elements of the same data type stored in contiguous memory locations.

Example:

int arr [5] = {1, 2, 3, 4, 5}; // Array of integers

char name[10] = "John"; // Array of characters (string)

Pointer:

A variable that stores the memory address of another variable.

Example:

```
int a = 10;
int *ptr = &a; // Pointer to an integer
```

Function:

Functions in C are also considered derived data types, as they take input and return values of specific data types.

Example:

```
int sum(int a, int b)
{
return a + b;
}
```

Example:

```
#include <stdio.h>
int main ()
{
int a = 10; // Integer
float b = 3.14; // Floating-point
char c = 'A'; // Character
double d = 3.1415926535; // Double
unsigned int e = 25; // Unsigned Integer
printf ("int: %d\n", a);
printf ("float: %.2f\n", b);
printf ("char: %c\n", c);
printf ("double: %.10lf\n", d);
printf ("unsigned int: %u\n", e);
return 0;
}
```

Type conversion

Type conversion in C refers to converting one data type into another. It allows the manipulation of variables of different data types in a program.

There are two types of type conversion in C:

1. Implicit Type Conversion (Type Promotion):

Also known as type casting by the compiler.

The compiler automatically converts data types when assigning values of smaller data types to larger ones or during arithmetic operations.

Rules:

Lower to Higher Precision: Smaller data types (like int) are automatically promoted to larger types (like float or double).

Order of Promotion:

char → int → float → double → long double

Example:

```c
#include <stdio.h>
int main ()
{
int a = 5;
float b = 2.5;
float result = a + b; // 'a' is implicitly converted to float
printf ("Result: %.2f\n", result);
return 0;
}
```

Output:

Result: 7.50

2. Explicit Type Conversion (Type Casting):

Also known as manual type casting.

The programmer explicitly specifies the data type for conversion using the cast operator (type).

Syntax:

(type) value

Example:

```
#include <stdio.h>
int main () {
float a = 5.7;
int b = (int)a; // Explicitly cast float to int
printf ("Original: %.1f, After Casting: %d\n", a, b);
return 0;
}
```

Output:

Original: 5.7, After Casting: 5

When to Use Type Conversion:

To avoid type mismatch errors in expressions.

To suppress warnings when using mixed data types.

To perform precision control in computations.

CHAPTER IV

Header Files and Data Input and Output

Header Files

In C language, header files are files with a .h extension that contain declarations for functions, macros, constants, and data types. They allow code reuse and make it easier to manage large programs by separating declarations from implementation.

Purpose of Header Files

Function Declarations: Provide prototypes for library or user-defined functions.

Example: printf () is declared in stdio.h.

Macros and Constants: Define constants or macros using #define.

Example: #define PI 3.14159

Code Reuse: Allow sharing declarations across multiple .c files without rewriting code.

Types of Header Files

Standard Library Header Files:

These are provided by the C library.

Examples:

- stdio.h: For input/output functions like printf () and scanf ().
- stdlib.h: For memory allocation (malloc ()), conversions, etc.
- string.h: For string manipulation functions like strlen (), strcpy ().
- math.h: For mathematical operations like sqrt (), pow ().
- ctype.h: For character handling like isalpha (), isdigit ().

User-Defined Header Files:
Created by programmers to declare their own functions and constants.
Including Header Files
Use #include directive to include a header file in a program.
For standard library headers: < >
#include <stdio.h>

Advantages

Code Reusability: Avoid rewriting common code.
Modularity: Organize code into manageable pieces.
Ease of Maintenance: Modify code in the header file without changing all source files.

Formatted Input and Output functions

In C, formatted input and output functions are used to read data from or write data to the standard input/output (usually the keyboard and screen). These functions allow us to control how data is presented or read using format specifiers.

Formatted Input: scanf ()

Purpose:
scanf () is used to read formatted data from the standard input.

Syntax:
scanf ("format specifier", &variable);

Key Points:
The format specifier determines the type of data to read (e.g., integer, float, string).

The & operator (address-of) is required for all variables except strings.

Common format specifiers:
%d: Integer
%f: Float
%c: Character
%s: String (automatically adds a null character \0 at the end)

Example:

```c
#include <stdio.h>
int main () {
int num;
float price;
char letter;
printf ("Enter an integer, a float, and a character: ");
scanf ("%d %f %c", &num, &price, &letter);
printf ("You entered: %d, %.2f, %c\n", num, price, letter);
return 0;
}
```

Output:
Enter an integer, a float, and a character: 10 15.5 A

You entered: 10, 15.50, A

Formatted Output: printf()

Purpose:

printf () is used to display formatted data on the standard output.

Syntax:

printf ("format specifier", variable);

Key Points:

The format specifier determines how the data will be displayed.

Common format specifiers:

%d: Integer

%f: Float

%c: Character

%s: String

Formatting options can be added for precision, width, and alignment:

Width: Specifies the minimum number of characters to display (e.g., %5d for 5 characters wide).

Precision: Controls the number of decimal places for floating-point numbers (e.g., %.2f for 2 decimal places).

Example:

```c
#include <stdio.h>
int main () {
int num = 42;
float price = 19.99;
char letter = 'B';
printf ("Integer: %d\n", num);
printf ("Float: %.2f\n", price); // 2 decimal places
printf ("Character: %c\n", letter);
```

```c
printf ("Formatted: %-10d | %10.2f\n", num, price); // Alignment example
return 0;
}
```

Output:
Integer: 42
Float: 19.99
Character: B
Formatted: 42 | 19.99

Additional Features in scanf () and printf ()

For scanf ():
Reading multiple values:

```c
int a, b;
scanf ("%d %d", &a, &b); // Reads two integers
```

Skipping whitespace:

```c
char c;
scanf (" %c", &c); // Leading space skips any whitespace
```

Reading strings:

```c
char name[50];
scanf ("%s", name); // Reads a single word (no spaces)
```

For printf ():
Left-align with -:

```c
printf ("%-10d", 42); // Left-aligns within 10 spaces
```

Padding numbers:

```c
printf ("%05d", 42); // Pads with leading zeroes: 00042
```

Example: Combining Formatted Input and Output

```c
#include <stdio.h>
int main () {
int id;
float salary;
char name[30];
```

```
printf ("Enter your ID, salary, and name: ");
scanf ("%d %f %s", &id, &salary, name);
printf ("Employee Details:\n");
printf ("ID: %05d\n", id); // Padded with zeroes
printf ("Salary: %.2f\n", salary); // 2 decimal places
printf ("Name: %-10s\n", name); // Left-aligned
return 0;
}
```

Output:

Enter your ID, salary, and name: 101 5500.75 John
Employee Details:
ID: 00101
Salary: 5500.75
Name: John

Unformatted Input and Output functions

In C, unformatted input and output functions are used to handle raw or basic data without any formatting. These functions are simpler than formatted ones (scanf() and printf()) and are often used for handling characters, strings, or blocks of data.

Unformatted Input Functions

Unformatted input functions directly take data from the user or input source without interpreting it. The most common unformatted input functions are:

getchar ()

Reads a **single character** from the standard input (keyboard).

Returns the character read as an int.

Syntax:

```
char c = getchar ();
```

Example:
```c
#include <stdio.h>
int main ()
{
char ch;
printf ("Enter a character: ");
ch = getchar ();
printf ("You entered: %c\n", ch);
return 0;
}
```
Output:

Enter a character: A

You entered: A

gets () (Deprecated, Unsafe)

Reads an entire string from standard input (until a newline character is encountered).

Adds a null character (\0) at the end of the string.

Avoid using gets () because it does not check for buffer overflow. Use fgets () instead.

Syntax:
```c
char str[50];
gets(str);
```
Example (use cautiously):
```c
#include <stdio.h>
int main () {
char name[50];
printf ("Enter your name: ");
gets(name);
printf ("Hello, %s!\n", name);
return 0;
}
```
fgets () (Recommended Alternative to gets ())

Reads a line of text, including spaces, up to a specified length or until a newline is encountered.

Syntax:

fgets (string, size, stdin);

Example:

```
#include <stdio.h>
int main () {
char name [50];
printf ("Enter your name: ");
fgets (name, 50, stdin); // Reads up to 49 characters
printf ("Hello, %s", name); // Includes the newline character
return 0;
}
```

Unformatted Output Functions

Unformatted output functions directly write raw data to the standard output without any formatting. The most common unformatted output functions are:

putchar ()

Writes a single character to the standard output (screen).

Returns the character written as an int.

Syntax:

putchar(character);

Example:

```
#include <stdio.h>
int main () {
char ch = 'B';
printf ("The character is: ");
putchar(ch);
putchar('\n'); // Adds a newline
```

```c
return 0;
}
```
Output:
The character is: B
puts ()
Writes a string to the standard output followed by a newline.
Syntax:
```c
puts(string);
```
Example:
```c
#include <stdio.h>
int main () {
char message [] = "Hello, world!";
puts(message); // Automatically adds a newline
return 0;
}
```
Output:
Hello, world!
Example: Combining Unformatted Input and Output
```c
#include <stdio.h>
int main () {
char name [50];
char initial;
// Using fgets () for input
printf ("Enter your name: ");
fgets (name, 50, stdin);
// Using getchar () for input
printf ("Enter the initial of your last name: ");
initial = getchar ();
// Output using puts () and putchar ()
printf ("Hello, ");
puts(name); // Outputs the name with a newline
printf ("Your last name starts with: ");
```

```
putchar(initial);
putchar('\n'); // Adds a newline
return 0;
}
```

Output:

Enter your name: John Doe

Enter the initial of your last name: D

Hello, John Doe

Your last name starts with: D

CHAPTER V

Operators, Expression and Statements

Operator

An operator is a symbol or keyword in C that tells the compiler to perform a specific operation on operands.
Example: +, -, *, /, = are operators.

Operand

An operand is the value or variable on which the operator performs the operation.
Example: In the expression a + b, a and b are operands.

Operation

An operation is the process performed by the operator on the operands to produce a result.
Example: In the expression a + b, the addition (+) is the operation performed between a and b.

Example
```c
#include <stdio.h>
int main () {
int a = 5; // Operand
int b = 3; // Operand
int result ; // Operand to store the result
result = a + b; // '+' is the operator, and 'a + b' is the operation
printf ("The result of %d + %d = %d\n", a, b, result);
```

```
return 0;
}
```
Output:

The result of 5 + 3 = 8

Explanation

Operator: + performs the addition.

Operands: a and b are the values being added.

Operation: The addition of a and b results in 8.

In C, operators are symbols or keywords used to perform specific operations on variables or values. They enable calculations, comparisons, logical decisions, and more. Operators act on operands (data items like variables, constants, or expressions) to produce a result.

Operators in C

	Operators	Type
Unary Operator	++, --	Unary Operator
Binary Operator	+, -, *, /, %	Arithmetic Operator
	<, <=, >, >=, ==, !=	Rational Operator
	&&, ||, !	Logical Operator
	&, |, <<, >>, ~, ^	Bitwise Operator
	=, +=, -=, *=, /=, %=	Assignment Operator
Ternary Operator	?:	Ternary or Conditional Operator

Operators in C

Types of Operators in C

Arithmetic Operators

// C program to illustrate the arithmetic operators

```c
#include <stdio.h>
    int main ()
    {
    int a = 25, b = 5;
    // using operators and printing results
    printf ("a + b = %d\n", a + b);
    printf ("a - b = %d\n", a - b);
    printf ("a * b = %d\n", a * b);
    printf ("a / b = %d\n", a / b);
    printf ("a % b = %d\n", a % b);
    printf ("+a = %d\n", +a);
    printf ("-a = %d\n", -a);
    printf ("a++ = %d\n", a++);
    printf ("a-- = %d\n", a--);
    return 0;
    }
```

Output
```
a + b = 30
a - b = 20
a * b = 125
a / b = 5
a % b = 0
+a = 25
-a = -25
```

a++ = 25

a-- = 26

Relational (Comparison) Operators

Used to compare two values. They return 1 (true) or 0 (false).

```c
// C program to illustrate the relational operators
#include <stdio.h>
int main ()
{
int a = 25, b = 5;
// using operators and printing results
printf ("a < b : %d\n", a < b);
printf ("a > b : %d\n", a > b);
printf ("a <= b: %d\n", a <= b);
printf ("a >= b: %d\n", a >= b);
printf ("a == b: %d\n", a == b);
printf ("a != b : %d\n", a != b);
return 0;
}
```

Output

a < b : 0

a > b : 1

a <= b: 0

a >= b: 1

a == b: 0

a != b : 1

Logical Operators

Used to combine multiple conditions or perform logical operations. They return 1 (true) or 0 (false).

```c
// C program to illustrate the logical operators
#include <stdio.h>
int main ()
{
int a = 25, b = 5;
// using operators and printing results
printf ("a && b : %d\n", a && b);
printf ("a || b : %d\n", a || b);
printf ("!a: %d\n", !a);
return 0;
}
a && b : 1
a || b : 1
!a: 0
```

Bitwise Operators

Operate on the binary representation of data.

```c
// C program to illustrate the bitwise operators
#include <stdio.h>
int main ()
{
int a = 25, b = 5;
// using operators and printing results
printf ("a & b: %d\n", a & b);
printf ("a | b: %d\n", a | b);
printf ("a ^ b: %d\n", a ^ b);
printf ("~a: %d\n", ~a);
printf ("a >> b: %d\n", a >> b);
printf ("a << b: %d\n", a << b);
return 0;
}
```

Output

a & b: 1
a | b: 29
a ^ b: 28
~a: -26
a >> b: 0
a << b: 800

Assignment Operators

Used to assign values to variables.

```c
// C program to illustrate the assignment operators
#include <stdio.h>
int main ()
{
int a = 25, b = 5;
// using operators and printing results
printf ("a = b: %d\n", a = b);
printf ("a += b: %d\n", a += b);
printf ("a -= b: %d\n", a -= b);
printf ("a *= b: %d\n", a *= b);
printf ("a /= b: %d\n", a /= b);
printf ("a %%= b: %d\n", a %= b);
printf ("a &= b: %d\n", a &= b);
printf ("a |= b: %d\n", a |= b);
printf ("a >>= b: %d\n", a >>= b);
printf ("a <<= b: %d\n", a <<= b);
return 0;
}
```

Output:
a = b: 5
a += b: 10
a -= b: 5
a *= b: 25

a /= b: 5

a %= b: 0

a &= b: 0

a |= b: 5

a >>= b: 0

a <<= b: 0

Increment and Decrement Operators

Used to increase or decrease a value by 1.

```c
// C program to illustrate increment
#include <stdio.h>
int main ()
{
int a = 5;
int b = 5;
int c=a++;
int p=++b;
printf ("Pre-Incrementing p = %d \tb=%d\n",p,b );
printf ("Post-Incrementing c = %d\ta=%d", c,a);
return 0;
}
```

Output: Pre-Incrementing p =6 b=6

Post-Incrementing c =5 a=6

```c
// C program to illustrate decrement
#include <stdio.h>
int main ()
{
int a = 5;
int b = 5;
printf ("Pre-Decrementing a = %d\n", --a);
printf ("Post-Decrementing b = %d", b--);
return 0;
```

```
}
```
Output: Pre-Decrementing a =4
Post-Decrementing b=4

sizeof ()

This operator returns the size of its operand, in bytes. The sizeof() operator always precedes its operand. The operand is an expression, or it may be a cast.

Below is the implementation of sizeof () operator:

```c
// C program to illustrate the sizeof operator
#include <stdio.h>
#include <stdio.h>
int main ()
{
// printing the size of double and int using sizeof
printf ("Size of double: %d\n", sizeof(double));
printf ("Size of int: %d\n", sizeof(int));
return 0;
}
```

Output:
Size of double: 8
Size of int: 4

Conditional (Ternary) Operator

A shorthand for if-else statements.

```c
Syntax: condition ? expression1 : expression2;
Example:
int a = 10, b = 5, max;
max = (a > b) ? a : b; // Returns `a` if condition is true,
otherwise `b`
printf ("Max = %d", max); // Output: Max = 10
```

Example:

```c
#include <stdio.h>
int main ()
{ int num1, num2, max;
// Input two numbers
printf ("Enter two numbers: ");
scanf ("%d %d", &num1, &num2);
// Find the maximum using the ternary operator
max = (num1 > num2) ? num1 : num2;
// Output the result
printf ("The larger number is: %d\n", max);
return 0;
}
```

Special Operators

Example Program: Using Different Operators

```c
#include <stdio.h>
int main () {
int a = 10, b = 3, max;
float result;
// Arithmetic Operators
result = a / b; // Integer division
printf ("Arithmetic: %d %% %d = %d\n", a, b, a % b);
// Relational Operators
printf ("Relational: a > b = %d\n", a > b);
// Logical Operators
printf ("Logical: (a > b) && (b > 0) = %d\n", (a > b) &&
(b > 0));
// Bitwise Operators
printf ("Bitwise: a & b = %d\n", a & b);
```

```
// Ternary Operator
max = (a > b) ? a : b;
printf ("Ternary: Max = %d\n", max);
return 0;
}
```

Output:

```
Arithmetic: 10 % 3 = 1
Relational: a > b = 1
Logical: (a > b) && (b > 0) = 1
Bitwise: a & b = 2
Ternary: Max = 10
```

Expression

In C language, an expression is a combination of variables, constants, operators, and function calls that are evaluated to produce a value.

Simple Expressions: Direct values or variables.

Example: 5, a

1. Arithmetic Expressions: Use arithmetic operators like +, -, *, /.

Example: a + b * c

2. Relational Expressions: Compare values using relational operators like >, <, ==, etc.

Example: a > b

3. Logical Expressions: Combine conditions with logical operators like &&, ||, !.

Example: (a > b) && (c != d)

4. Assignment Expressions: Assign values to variables using =.

Example: x = a + b

5. Function Call Expressions: Involve calling a function. Example: sum (a, b)

Statement:- In C language, a statement is an instruction that the compiler can execute. It performs an action, such as assigning a value, controlling program flow, or performing a calculation.

Types of Statements:

1. Expression Statements: Ends with a semicolon and typically performs an operation.

Example: x = 5;, a++;

2. Compound Statements: A block of statements enclosed in { }, treated as a single unit.

Example:

```
{
int x = 10;
printf ("%d", x);
}
```

3. Control Statements: Direct the flow of execution.

Conditional Statements: if, if-else, switch.

Example: if (x > 0) printf("Positive");

4. Looping Statements: for, while, do-while.

Example: for (int i = 0; i < 5; i++) printf("%d", i);

5. Jump Statements: break, continue, goto, return.

Example: return 0;

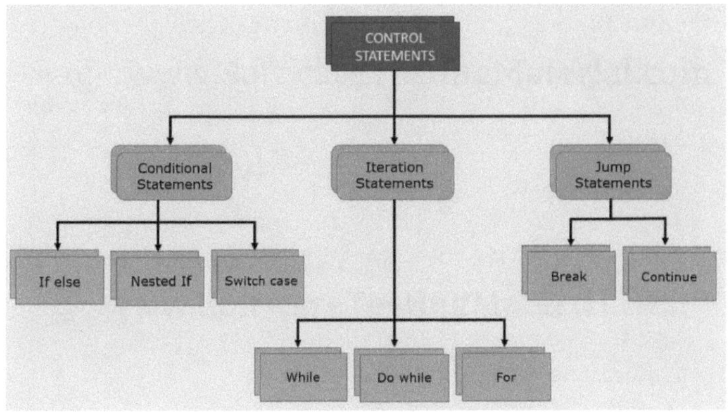

Control Statements

Precedence and Associativity in C Language

Operator Precedence

Precedence determines the order in which operators are evaluated in an expression. Operators with higher precedence are evaluated before those with lower precedence.

For example:

int x = 5 + 3 * 2; // 3 * 2 is evaluated first, then +5

Here, * (multiplication) has a higher precedence than + (addition), so the result is 11.

Operator Associativity

Associativity determines the order in which operators of the same precedence are evaluated. It can be:

Left to Right (most operators follow this)

Right to Left (used for assignment and some unary operators)

For example:

int y = 10 / 2 * 3; // Left to right: (10 / 2) * 3 = 15

Since / and * have the same precedence and left-to-right associativity, division happens first.

Example:

Understanding of Precedence

```c
#include <stdio.h>
int main ()
{
int result = 10 + 5 * 2; // Multiplication (*) happens first
printf ("%d", result); // Output: 20
return 0;
}
```

Example:

Understanding Associativity

```c
#include <stdio.h>
int main () {
int a = 10, b = 5, c = 2;
int result = a - b - c; // (10 - 5) - 2 (Left to Right)
printf ("%d", result); // Output: 3
return 0;
}
```

71

CHAPTER VI

Decision Making/Selective/ Conditional Statements

In C language, decision-making statements help to control the flow of execution based on certain conditions. These statements allow the program to take different paths based on the results of logical or relational expressions.

if Statement

Executes a block of code if the condition is true.
Syntax:

```
if (condition) {
// Code to execute if the condition is true
}
```

Example:

```
if (x > 0)
{
printf ("x is positive.");
}
// C program to illustrate If statement
#include <stdio.h>
int main ()
{
int i = 10;
if (i > 15)
{
printf("10 is greater than 15");
```

```
}
printf ("I am Not in if");
}
```

Output

I am Not in if

if-else Statement

Executes one block of code if the condition is true and another if the condition is false.

```
Syntax:
if (condition)
{
// Code if condition is true
}
else
{
// Code if condition is false
}
Example:
if (x % 2 == 0)
{
printf ("x is even.");
}
else
{
printf ("x is odd.");
}
// C program to illustrate If statement
#include <stdio.h>
int main ()
{
int i = 20;
```

```c
if (i < 15) {
printf("i is smaller than 15");
}
else {
printf ("i is greater than 15");
}
return 0;
}
```

Output

i is greater than 15

else if Ladder

Used to test multiple conditions sequentially.

```c
Syntax:
if (condition1)
{
// Code if condition1 is true
}
else if (condition2)
{
// Code if condition2 is true
}
else
{
// Code if none of the above conditions are true
}
Example:
if (x > 0)
{
printf("x is positive.");
}
else if (x < 0)
```

```c
{
printf("x is negative.");
}
else
{
printf("x is zero.");
}
// C program to illustrate nested-if statement
#include <stdio.h>
int main ()
{
int i = 20;
if (i == 10)
printf ("i is 10");
else if (i == 15)
printf ("i is 15");
else if (i == 20)
printf ("i is 20");
else
printf ("i is not present");
}
Output: i is 20
```

Nested if

An if statement inside another if statement.

```c
Syntax:
if (condition1)
{
if (condition2)
{
// Code if both condition1 and condition2 are true
}
```

```c
}
Example:
if (x > 0) {
if (x % 2 == 0)
{
printf ("x is positive and even.");
}
}
// C program to illustrate nested-if statement
#include <stdio.h>
int main ()
{
int i = 10;
if (i == 10) {
// First if statement
if (i < 15)
printf ("i is smaller than 15\n");
// Nested - if statement
// Will only be executed if statement above
// is true
if (i < 12)
printf("i is smaller than 12 too\n");
else
printf("i is greater than 15");
}
else {
if (i == 20) {
// Nested - if statement
// Will only be executed if statement above
// is true
if (i < 22)
printf("i is smaller than 22 too\n");
else
```

```c
printf("i is greater than 25");
}
}
return 0;
}
```

Output

i is smaller than 15

i is smaller than 12 too

Switch Statement

Used when there are multiple possible values for a variable. It is a better alternative to an if-else ladder in such cases.

```c
Syntax:
switch (expression)
{
case value1:
// Code to execute if expression == value1
break;
case value2:
// Code to execute if expression == value2
break;
...
default:
// Code to execute if no case matches
}
```

```c
Example:
switch (day) {
case 1:
printf("Monday");
break;
case 2:
printf("Tuesday");
```

```c
break;
default:
printf("Invalid day");
}
// C Program to illustrate the use of switch statement
#include <stdio.h>
int main()
{
// variable to be used in switch statement
int var = 2;
// declaring switch cases
switch (var) {
case 1:
printf("Case 1 is executed");
break;
case 2:
printf("Case 2 is executed");
break;
default: printf("Default Case is executed");
break;
}
return 0;
}
```

Output: Case 2 is executed

Points:

Curly braces {} are optional for single-line statements but recommended for clarity.

The break keyword in a switch prevents fall-through to the next case.

Always include a default case in a switch for completeness.

Use else if to avoid excessive nesting of if statements.

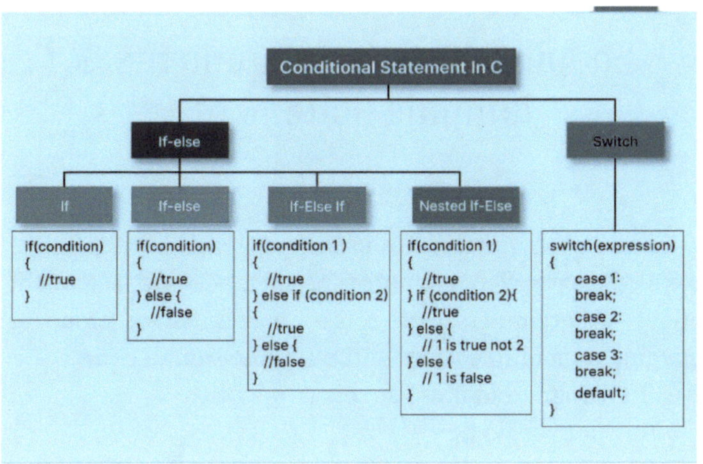

Condition Statement in C

CHAPTER VII

Looping/Iterative Statements & Jumping Statements

Loops in programming are used to repeat a block of code until the specified condition is met. A loop statement allows programmers to execute a statement or group of statements multiple times without repetition of code.

```c
// C program to illustrate need of loops
#include <stdio.h>
int main ()
{
printf( "Hello World\n");
printf( "Hello World\n");
printf( "Hello World\n");
printf( "Hello World\n");
printf( "Hello World\n");
printf( "Hello World\n");
printf( "Hello World\n");
printf( "Hello World\n");
printf( "Hello World\n");
printf( "Hello World\n");
return 0;
}
```

Output
Hello World
Hello World
Hello World
Hello World
Hello World

Hello World
Hello World
Hello World
Hello World
Hello World

There are mainly two types of loops in C Programming:

1. **Entry Controlled loops:** In Entry controlled loops the test condition is checked before entering the main body of the loop. For Loop and While Loop is Entry-controlled loops.

2. **Exit Controlled loops:** In Exit controlled loops the test condition is evaluated at the end of the loop body. The loop body will execute at least once, irrespective of whether the condition is true or false. do-while Loop is Exit Controlled loop.

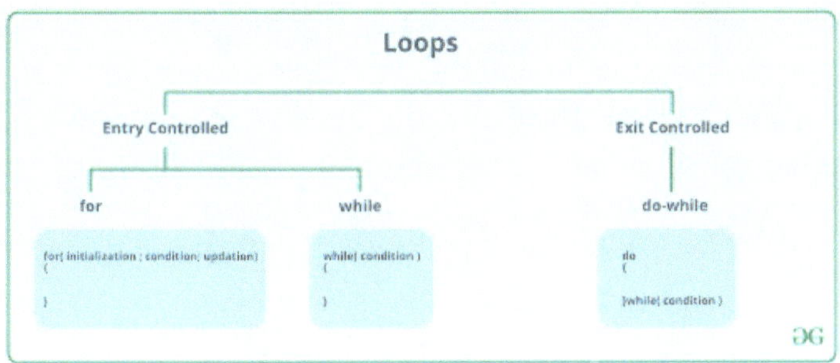

for Loop

for loop in C programming is a repetition control structure that allows programmers to write a loop that will be executed a specific number of times. for loop enables programmers to perform n number of steps together in a single line.

Syntax:

for (initialize expression; test expression; update expression)
{
//
// body of for loop
//
}

Example:

for (int i = 0; i < n; ++i)
{
printf ("Body of for loop which will execute till n");
}

In for loop, a loop variable is used to control the loop. Firstly, we initialize the loop variable with some value, then check its test condition. If the statement is true then control will move to the body and the body of for loop will be executed. Steps will be repeated till the exit condition becomes true. If the test condition will be false then it will stop.

Initialization Expression: In this expression, we assign a loop variable or loop counter to some value. for example: int i=1;

Test Expression: In this expression, test conditions are performed. If the condition evaluates to true then the loop body will be executed and then an update of the loop variable is done. If the test expression becomes false then the control will exit from the loop. for example, i<=9;

Update Expression: After execution of the loop body loop variable is updated by some value it could be incremented, decremented, multiplied, or divided by any value.

Example:
```c
// C program to illustrate for loop
#include <stdio.h>
int main ()
{
int i = 0;
for (i = 1; i <= 10; i++)
{
printf ( "Hello World\n");
}
return 0;
}
```

Output
```
Hello World
Hello World
Hello World
Hello World
Hello World
Hello World
Hello World
Hello World
Hello World
Hello World
```

While Loop

While loop does not depend upon the number of iterations. In for loop the number of iterations was previously known to us but in the While loop, the execution is terminated on the basis of the test condition. If the test condition will become false then it will break from the while loop else body will be executed.

Syntax:
initialization_expression;

while (test_expression)
{
// body of the while loop

update_expression;
}

```c
// C program to illustrate while loop
#include <stdio.h>
int main ()
{
// Initialization expression
int i = 2;
// Test expression
while(i < 10)
{
// loop body
printf ( "Hello World\n");
// update expression
i++;
}
return 0;
}
```

Output
Hello World
Hello World

Hello World
Hello World
Hello World
Hello World
Hello World
Hello World

do-while Loop

The do-while loop is similar to a while loop but the only difference lies in the do-while loop test condition which is tested at the end of the body. In the do-while loop, the loop body will execute at least once irrespective of the test condition.

Syntax:

```
initialization_expression;
do
{
// body of do-while loop


update_expression;

} while (test_expression);
    // C program to illustrate do-while loop
    #include <stdio.h>
    int main ()
    {
    // Initialization expression
    int i = 2;
    do
    {
    // loop body
```

```c
printf ( "Hello World\n");
// Update expression
i++;
// Test expression
} while (i < 1);
return 0;
}
```

Output

Hello World

Above program will evaluate (i<1) as false since i = 2. But still, as it is a do-while loop the body will be executed once.

Infinite Loop

An infinite loop is executed when the test expression never becomes false and the body of the loop is executed repeatedly. A program is stuck in an Infinite loop when the condition is always true. Mostly this is an error that can be resolved by using Loop Control statements.

Using for loop:

```c
// C program to demonstrate infinite loops using for loop
#include <stdio.h>
int main ()
{
int i;
for ( ; ; )
{
printf("This loop will run forever.\n");
}
return 0;
```

```
}
```

Output

```
    This loop will run forever.
This loop will run forever.
This loop will run forever.
...
```

Using While loop:

```c
// C program to demonstrate infinite loop using while
#include <stdio.h>
int main ()
{
while (1)
printf ("This loop will run forever.\n");
return 0;
}
```

Output

```
    This loop will run forever.
This loop will run forever.
This loop will run forever.
...
```

Using the do-while loop:

```c
// C program to demonstrate infinite loop using do-while
    #include <stdio.h>
    int main ()
    {
    do
    {
    printf ("This loop will run forever.\n");
    } while (1);
```

```
    return 0;
}
```
Output

This loop will run forever.
This loop will run forever.
This loop will run forever.

Jump Statements

Jump control statements in C programming are used to change execution from its normal sequence.

Jump Statements in C

In C, jump statements are used to jump from one part of the code to another altering the normal flow of the program. They are used to transfer the program control to somewhere else in the program.

Types of Jump Statements in C

There are 4 types of jump statements in C:

1. break
2. continue
3. goto
4. return

break

The break statement exits or terminates the loop or switch statement based on a certain condition, without executing the remaining code.

Syntax of break

break;
Uses of break

- The break statement is used in C for the following purposes:
- To come out of the loop.
- To come out from the nested loops.
- To come out of the switch case.

Example of break Statement

The statements inside the loop are executed sequentially. When the break statement is encountered within the loop and the condition for the break statement becomes true, the program flow breaks out of the loop, regardless of any remaining iterations.

```c
// C program to illustrate the break in c loop
#include <stdio.h>
int main()
{
int i;
// for loop
for (i = 1; i <= 10; i++)
{
// when i = 6, the loop should end
if (i == 6)
{
break;
}
printf("%d ", i);
}
printf("Loop exited.\n");
return 0;
}
```

Output

1 2 3 4 5 Loop exited.

Explanation:

Loop Execution Starts and goes normally till i = 5.

When i = 6, the condition for the break statement becomes true and the program control immediately exits the loop.

The control continues with the remaining statements outside the loop.

continue

The continue statement in C is used to skip the remaining code after the continue statement within a loop and jump to the next iteration of the loop. When the continue statement is encountered, the loop control immediately jumps to the next iteration, by skipping the lines of code written after it within the loop body.

Syntax of continue

continue;

Example of continue Statement

```c
// C Program to illustrate the continue statement
#include <stdio.h>
int main()
{
int i;
// loop
for (i = 0; i < 5; i++) {
if (i == 2) {
// continue to be executed if i = 2
printf("Skipping iteration %d\n", i);
continue;
}
```

```c
        printf("Executing iteration %d\n", i);
    }
    return 0;
}
```

Output

Executing iteration 0

Executing iteration 1

Skipping iteration 2

Executing iteration 3

Executing iteration 4

Explanation: The for loop iterates from 0 to 4. Inside the loop, we check if i is equal to 2. If the condition is true, the continue statement is executed, and it skips the remaining code within the loop for that iteration. If the condition is false, the code proceeds normally.

goto Statement

The goto statement is used to jump to a specific point from anywhere in a function. It is used to transfer the program control to a labeled statement within the same function.

Syntax of goto Statement

goto label;

.

.

label:

//code

Example of goto Statement

Check if a number is odd or even using goto statement.

C++

// C program to check if a number is even or not using goto statement

#include <stdio.h>

```c
// function to check even or not
void checkEvenOrNot(int num)
{
if (num % 2 == 0)
// jump to even
goto even;
else
// jump to odd
goto odd;
even:
printf("%d is even", num);
// return if even
return;
odd:
printf("%d is odd", num);
}
int main()
{
int num = 26;
checkEvenOrNot(num);
return 0;
}
```

Output

26 is even

return Statement

The return statement in C is used to terminate the execution of a function and return a value to the caller. It is commonly used to provide a result back to the calling code.

```c
return expression;
```

Example

```c
#include <stdio.h>
int add(int a, int b)
{
```

```c
int sum = a + b;
return sum; // Return the sum as the result of the
// function
}
void printMessage()
{
printf("welcome\n");
return; // Return from the function with no value
(void)
}
int main()
{
int result = add(5, 3);
printf("Result: %d\n", result);
printMessage();
return 0;
}
```

Output

```
Result: 8
welcome
```

CHAPTER VIII

Programs

//Program to Display "Hello"

```c
#include <stdio.h>
   int main()
   {
   // printf() displays the string inside quotation
   printf("Hello");
   return 0;
   }
   Output
   Hello
```

// Program to Print message using escape sequence characters

```c
#include <stdio.h>
   int main() {
   // Printing your name "Rahul" on the output screen
   printf("Rahul\nGupta");
   return 0;
   }
   Output
   Rahul
   Gupta
```

// Program to Print Integer value

```c
#include <stdio.h>
int main()
{
// Declaring integer
int x = 5;
// Printing values
printf("Printing Integer value %d", x);
return 0;
}
```

Output

Printing Integer value 5

// C program to print ASCII Value of Character using implicit conversion with format specifier.

```c
#include <stdio.h>
int main ()
{
char c = 'k';
// %d displays the integer value of
// a character
// %c displays the actual character
printf("The ASCII value of %c is %d", c, c);
return 0;
}
```

Output

The ASCII value of k is 107

// Program to Swap Two Numbers using 3rd Variable

```c
#include <stdio.h>
    int main () {
    int a = 5, b = 10, temp;
    // Swapping values of a and b
    temp = a;
    a = b;
    b = temp;
    printf("a = %d, b = %d\n", a, b);
    return 0;
    }
```
Output
```
a = 10, b = 5
```

// Program to convert Fahrenheit temperature to Celsius temperature

```c
#include <stdio.h>
    int main()
    {
    float fahrenheit, celsius;
    // Input temperature in Fahrenheit
    printf("Enter temperature in Fahrenheit: ");
    scanf("%f", &fahrenheit);
    // Output the result
    printf("Temperature in Celsius: %.2f°C\n", celsius);
    return 0;
    }
```
Outputs:
```
Enter temperature in Fahrenheit: 98.6
Temperature in Celsius: 37.00°C
```

// C Program to Find the Size of int, float, double, and char using sizeof operator directly

```c
#include <stdio.h>
   int main()
   {
   // Determine and Print the size of int
   printf("Size of int: %u bytes\n", sizeof(int));
   // Determine and Print the size of float
   printf("Size of float: %u bytes\n", sizeof(float));
   // Determine and Print the size of double
   printf("Size of double: %u bytes\n", sizeof(double));
   // Determine and Print the size of char
   printf("Size of char: %u bytes\n", sizeof(char));
   return 0;
   }
```

Output
Size of int: 4 bytes
Size of float: 4 bytes
Size of double: 8 bytes
Size of char: 1 bytes

// C program to find the simple interest

```c
#include <stdio.h>
   int main()
   {
   // Input values
   float P = 1, R = 1, T = 1;
   // Calculate simple interest
   float SI = (P * T * R) / 100;
```

```c
// Print Simple Interest
printf("Simple Interest = %f\n", SI);
return 0;
}
```

Output

Simple Interest = 0.010000

// C program to calculate Compound Interest

```c
#include <stdio.h>
#include<math.h>
int main()
{
// Principal amount
double principal = 10000;
// Annual rate of interest
double rate = 5;
// Time
double time = 2;
// Calculating compound Interest
double Amount = principal * ((pow((1 + rate / time))));
double CI = Amount - principal;
printf("Compound Interest is : %lf",CI);
return 0;
}
```

Output:

Compound interest is 1025

// C program to demonstrate the area and perimeter of rectangle

```c
#include <stdio.h>
```

```c
int main()
{
int l = 10, b = 10;
printf("Area of rectangle is : %d", l * b);
printf("\nPerimeter of rectangle is : %d", 2 * (l + b));
return 0;
}
```

Output

Area of rectangle is : 100

Perimeter of rectangle is : 40

//C program to calculate the total marks and percentage of a student in 5 subjects:

```c
#include <stdio.h>
   int main()
   {
   float sub1, sub2, sub3, sub4, sub5, total, percentage;
   // Input marks for 5 subjects
   printf("Enter marks for 5 subjects: ");
   scanf("%f %f %f %f %f", &sub1, &sub2, &sub3, &sub4, &sub5);
   // Calculate total and percentage
   total = sub1 + sub2 + sub3 + sub4 + sub5;
   percentage = (total / 500) * 100; // Assuming each
subject is out of 100
   // Display results
   printf("\nTotal Marks = %.2f", total);
   printf("\nPercentage = %.2f%%\n", percentage);
   return 0;
   }
```

Output:
Enter marks for 5 subjects: 85 90 78 88 95
Total Marks = 436.00
Percentage = 87.20%

//program of swapping of two numbers without using 3rd variable

```c
#include <stdio.h>
int main()
{
int a, b;
// Input two numbers
printf("Enter two numbers: ");
scanf("%d %d", &a, &b);
printf("\nBefore swapping: a = %d, b = %d\n", a, b);
// Swap without using a third variable
a = a + b;
b = a - b;
a = a - b;
printf("After swapping: a = %d, b = %d\n", a, b);
return 0;
}
```

Output:
Enter two numbers: 5 8
Before swapping: a = 5, b = 8
After swapping: a = 8, b = 5

//Program to Check if a Number is Positive, Negative, or Zero (if-else)

```c
#include <stdio.h>
int main()
```

```c
{
int num;
// Input a number
printf("Enter a number: ");
scanf("%d", &num);
// Decision making using if-else
if (num > 0)
printf("The number is Positive.\n");
else if (num < 0)
printf("The number is Negative.\n");
else
printf("The number is Zero.\n");
return 0;
}
```

Output:

Enter a number: -5
The number is Negative.

//Program to find the Largest of Three Numbers (Nested if)

```c
#include <stdio.h>
int main()
{
int a, b, c;
// Input three numbers
printf("Enter three numbers: ");
scanf("%d %d %d", &a, &b, &c);
// Nested if decision making
if (a >= b)
{
if (a >= c)
```

```c
printf("Largest number is %d\n", a);
else
printf("Largest number is %d\n", c);
}
else
{
if (b >= c)
printf("Largest number is %d\n", b);
else
printf("Largest number is %d\n", c);
}
return 0;
}
```

Output:
Enter three numbers: 12 45 30
Largest number is 45

//Program to Check if a Number is Even or Odd (if-else)

```c
#include <stdio.h>
int main()
{
int num;
// Input a number
printf("Enter a number: ");
scanf("%d", &num);
// Using if-else decision making
if (num % 2 == 0)
printf("%d is Even.\n", num);
else
printf("%d is Odd.\n", num);
return 0;
```

```
}
```
Output:
Enter a number: 9
9 is Odd.

//Program of Grade Calculation Using Else-if Ladder

```c
#include <stdio.h>
int main()
{
int marks;
// Input marks
printf("Enter your marks: ");
scanf("%d", &marks);
// Using else-if ladder to assign grades
if (marks >= 90)
printf("Grade: A\n");
else if (marks >= 80)
printf("Grade: B\n");
else if (marks >= 70)
printf("Grade: C\n");
else if (marks >= 60)
printf("Grade: D\n");
else
printf("Grade: F\n");
return 0;
}
```
Output:
Enter your marks: 85
Grade: B

//*Program of Simple Calculator Using Switch Statement*

```c
#include <stdio.h>
    int main()
    {
    char op;
    double num1, num2, result;
    // Input operator and numbers
    printf("Enter an operator (+, -, *, /): ");
    scanf(" %c", &op);
    printf("Enter two numbers: ");
    scanf("%lf %lf", &num1, &num2);
    // Switch-case decision making
    switch (op)
    {
    case '+':
    result = num1 + num2;
    printf("Result = %.2lf\n", result);
    break;
    case '-':
    result = num1 - num2;
    printf("Result = %.2lf\n", result);
    break;
    case '*':
    result = num1 * num2;
    printf("Result = %.2lf\n", result);
    break;
    case '/':
    if (num2 != 0)
    printf("Result = %.2lf\n", num1 / num2);
    else
    printf("Error! Division by zero.\n");
```

```c
break;
default:
printf("Invalid operator!\n");
}
return 0;
}
```

Output:
```
Enter an operator (+, -, *, /): *
Enter two numbers: 5 3
Result = 15.00
```

// Program to check whether a given year is a leap year or not .

```c
#include <stdio.h>
int main()
{
int year;
// Input year from user
printf("Enter a year: ");
scanf("%d", &year);
// Leap year conditions
if ((year % 4 == 0 && year % 100 != 0) || (year % 400 == 0))
printf("%d is a Leap Year.\n", year);
else
printf("%d is Not a Leap Year.\n", year);
return 0;
}
```

Output 1
```
Enter a year: 2024
2024 is a Leap Year.
Output 2 (Not a Leap Year)
```

Enter a year: 2023
2023 is Not a Leap Year.

// Program to check whether a shopkeeper is in profit or loss

```c
#include <stdio.h>
int main()
{
float cost_price, selling_price, profit_or_loss;
// Input cost price and selling price
printf("Enter Cost Price: ");
scanf("%f", &cost_price);
printf("Enter Selling Price: ");
scanf("%f", &selling_price);
// Calculate profit or loss
profit_or_loss = selling_price - cost_price;
// Decision making
if (profit_or_loss > 0)
printf("Profit of %.2f\n", profit_or_loss);
else if (profit_or_loss < 0)
printf("Loss of %.2f\n", -profit_or_loss);
else
printf("No Profit, No Loss.\n");
return 0;
}
```

Outputs:
Case 1: Profit
Enter Cost Price: 500
Enter Selling Price: 700
Profit of 200.00
Case 2: Loss
Enter Cost Price: 600

Enter Selling Price: 400
Loss of 200.00
Case 3: No Profit, No Loss
Enter Cost Price: 300
Enter Selling Price: 300
No Profit, No Loss.

//*Program Using for Loop (Print Numbers from 1 to 10)*

```c
#include <stdio.h>
    int main()
    {
    int i;
    // Using for loop
    for (i = 1; i <= 10; i++)
    {
    printf("%d ", i);
    }
    return 0;
    }
```
Output:
1 2 3 4 5 6 7 8 9 10

//*Program Using while Loop (Sum of First 5 Natural Numbers)*

```c
#include <stdio.h>
    int main()
    {
    int i = 1, sum = 0;
    // Using while loop
```

```c
while (i <= 5) {
sum += i;
i++;
}
printf("Sum of first 5 natural numbers: %d\n", sum);
return 0;
}
```

Output:

Sum of first 5 natural numbers: 15

//Program Using do-while Loop (Print Numbers from 1 to 5)

```c
#include <stdio.h>
   int main()
   {
int i = 1;
// Using do-while loop
do {
printf("%d ", i);
i++;
} while (i <= 5);
return 0;
}
```

Output:

1 2 3 4 5

//Program Using for Loop to Print Multiplication Table of a Number

```c
#include <stdio.h>
   int main ()
   {
```

```c
int num, i;
// Input number
printf ("Enter a number: ");
scanf("%d", &num);
// Using for loop to print multiplication table
for (i = 1; i <= 10; i++) {
printf("%d x %d = %d\n", num, i, num * i);
}
return 0;
}
```

Output (for num = 3):

```
Enter a number: 3
3 x 1 = 3
3 x 2 = 6
3 x 3 = 9
3 x 4 = 12
3 x 5 = 15
3 x 6 = 18
3 x 7 = 21
3 x 8 = 24
3 x 9 = 27
3 x 10 = 30
```

//Program Using while Loop to Find Factorial of a Number

```c
#include <stdio.h>
int main()
{
int num, fact = 1, i = 1;
// Input number
printf("Enter a number: ");
scanf("%d", &num);
```

```c
// Using while loop to calculate factorial
while (i <= num)
{
fact *= i;
i++;
}
printf("Factorial of %d is %d\n", num, fact);
return 0;
}
```

Output (for num = 5):

Enter a number: 5

Factorial of 5 is 120

// Program to find the sum of the digits of a number, along with sample outputs.

```c
#include <stdio.h>
    int main()
    {
int num, sum = 0, digit;
// Input number from user
printf("Enter a number: ");
scanf("%d", &num);
// Process each digit and calculate sum
while (num != 0) {
digit = num % 10; // Extract last digit
sum += digit; // Add digit to sum
num /= 10; // Remove last digit
}
// Output result
printf("Sum of digits = %d\n", sum);
return 0;
```

```
}
```
Outputs:
Case 1:
Enter a number: 1234
Sum of digits = 10
Explanation: 1 + 2 + 3 + 4 = 10
Case 2:
Enter a number: 987
Sum of digits = 24
Explanation: 9 + 8 + 7 = 24

//Program to find the reverse of a number, along with sample outputs.

```c
#include <stdio.h>
    int main()
    {
    int num, reversed = 0, digit;
    // Input number from user
    printf("Enter a number: ");
    scanf("%d", &num);
    // Reverse the number
    while (num != 0) {
    digit = num % 10; // Extract last digit
    reversed = reversed * 10 + digit; // Add digit to reversed
number
    num /= 10; // Remove last digit
    }
    // Output the reversed number
    printf("Reversed number = %d\n", reversed);
    return 0;
    }
```
Outputs:

Case 1:

Enter a number: 1234

Reversed number = 4321

Explanation: The reverse of 1234 is 4321.

Case 2:

Enter a number: 90876

Reversed number = 67809

Explanation: The reverse of 90876 is 67809.

// Program to check whether a given number is a palindrome or not, along with sample outputs.

```c
#include <stdio.h>
    int main()
    {
    int num, reversed = 0, original, digit;
    // Input number from user
    printf("Enter a number: ");
    scanf("%d", &num);
    original = num; // Store the original number
    // Reverse the number
    while (num != 0) {
    digit = num % 10; // Extract last digit
    reversed = reversed * 10 + digit; // Add digit to reversed
number
    num /= 10; // Remove last digit
    }
    // Check if original and reversed numbers are equal
    if (original == reversed)
    printf("%d is a Palindrome.\n", original);
    else
    printf("%d is Not a Palindrome.\n", original)
```

```
return 0;
}
```

Outputs:

Case 1: Palindrome

Enter a number: 121

121 is a Palindrome.

Case 2: Not a Palindrome

Enter a number: 123

123 is Not a Palindrome.

// Program to check whether a given number is an Armstrong number or not, along with sample outputs.

```
#include <stdio.h>
    #include <math.h>
    int main()
    {
    int num, sum = 0, original, digit, count = 0;
    // Input number from user
    printf("Enter a number: ");
    scanf("%d", &num);
    original = num; // Store the original number
    // Count the number of digits in the number
    while (num != 0) {
    num /= 10;
    count++;
    }
    num = original; // Reset num to original value
    // Calculate the sum of each digit raised to the power of
'count'
    while (num != 0) {
    digit = num % 10; // Extract last digit
```

```c
sum += pow(digit, count); // Add digit raised to the power of 'count' to sum
num /= 10; // Remove last digit
}
// Check if sum is equal to the original number
if (sum == original)
printf("%d is an Armstrong number.\n", original);
else
printf("%d is Not an Armstrong number.\n", original);
return 0;
}
```

Outputs:

Case 1: Armstrong Number

Enter a number: 153

153 is an Armstrong number.

Explanation: 1^3 + 5^3 + 3^3 = 153, so 153 is an Armstrong number.

Case 2: Not an Armstrong Number

Enter a number: 123

123 is Not an Armstrong number.

Explanation: 1^3 + 2^3 + 3^3 = 36, so 123 is not an Armstrong number.

//Program to find the sum of the series 1 + 1/3 + 1/5 + 1/7 + ... using a do-while loop.

```c
#include <stdio.h>
int main()
{
int terms, i = 1;
double sum = 0.0;
// Input number of terms to sum
printf("Enter the number of terms: ");
```

```c
scanf("%d", &terms);
// Using do-while loop to calculate sum
do {
sum += 1.0 / i; // Add 1/i to the sum
i += 2; // Increment i by 2 to get the next odd number
} while (i <= (2 * terms - 1)); // Stop when i exceeds the
required number of terms
// Output the result
printf("Sum of the series: %.4f\n", sum);
return 0;
}
```

Output:

Case 1:

Enter the number of terms: 5

Sum of the series: 1.4636

Case 2:

Enter the number of terms: 7

Sum of the series: 1.7179

Output:

For 5 terms: 1 + 1/3 + 1/5 + 1/7 + 1/9 = 1.4636

For 7 terms: 1 + 1/3 + 1/5 + 1/7 + 1/9 + 1/11 + 1/13 = 1.7179

//Programs that print different patterns using nested for loops.

1. Right-Angled Triangle Pattern

```c
#include <stdio.h>
int main()
{
int i, j, rows;
```

```c
// Input number of rows
printf("Enter the number of rows: ");
scanf("%d", &rows);
// Nested for loop for the pattern
for (i = 1; i <= rows; i++) {
for (j = 1; j <= i; j++) {
printf("* ");
}
printf("\n");
}
return 0;
}
```

Output:

```
Enter the number of rows: 5
*
* *
* * *
* * * *
* * * * *
```

2. Inverted Right-Angled Triangle Pattern

```c
#include <stdio.h>
int main()
{
int i, j, rows;
// Input number of rows
printf("Enter the number of rows: ");
scanf("%d", &rows);
// Nested for loop for the inverted triangle pattern
for (i = rows; i >= 1; i--) {
for (j = 1; j <= i; j++) {
printf("* ");
```

```c
}
printf("\n");
}
return 0;
}
```

Output:

Enter the number of rows: 5

```
* * * * *
* * * *
* * *
* *
*
```

3. Pyramid Pattern

```c
#include <stdio.h>
int main()
{
int i, j, k, rows;
// Input number of rows
printf("Enter the number of rows: ");
scanf("%d", &rows);
// Nested for loop for the pyramid pattern
for (i = 1; i <= rows; i++) {
// Print spaces
for (j = i; j < rows; j++) {
printf(" ");
}
// Print stars
for (k = 1; k <= (2 * i - 1); k++) {
printf("*");
}
printf("\n");
```

```
}
return 0;
}
```

Output:

```
Enter the number of rows: 5
*
***
*****
*******
*********
```

4. Number Pyramid Pattern

```c
#include <stdio.h>
int main()
{
int i, j, k, rows;
// Input number of rows
printf("Enter the number of rows: ");
scanf("%d", &rows);
// Nested for loop for the number pyramid pattern
for (i = 1; i <= rows; i++) {
// Print spaces
for (j = i; j < rows; j++) {
printf(" ");
}
// Print numbers
for (k = 1; k <= (2 * i - 1); k++) {
printf("%d", k);
}
printf("\n");
}
```

```
return 0;
}
```

Output:

```
Enter the number of rows: 5
1
123
12345
1234567
123456789
```

5. Diamond Pattern

```c
#include <stdio.h>
int main()
{
int i, j, k, rows;
// Input number of rows
printf("Enter the number of rows: ");
scanf("%d", &rows);
// Upper half of diamond
for (i = 1; i <= rows; i++) {
// Print spaces
for (j = i; j < rows; j++) {
printf(" ");
}
// Print stars
for (k = 1; k <= (2 * i - 1); k++) {
printf("*");
}
printf("\n");
}
// Lower half of diamond
for (i = rows - 1; i >= 1; i--) {
// Print spaces
for (j = rows; j > i; j--) {
```

```c
printf(" ");
}
// Print stars
for (k = 1; k <= (2 * i - 1); k++) {
printf("*");
}
printf("\n");
}
return 0;
}
```

Output:

```
Enter the number of rows: 5
    *
   ***
  *****
 *******
*********
 *******
  *****
   ***
    *
```

//Program to check if a number is odd or even using the goto statement, along with sample output.

```c
#include <stdio.h>
int main()
{
int num;
// Input number from user
printf("Enter a number: ");
scanf("%d", &num);
```

```c
// Using goto statement to check if the number is even or odd
    if (num % 2 == 0)
    goto even; // If the number is even, jump to 'even' label
    else
    goto odd; // If the number is odd, jump to 'odd' label
    even:
    printf("%d is an Even number.\n", num);
    return 0;
    odd:
    printf("%d is an Odd number.\n", num);
    return 0;
    }
```

Output:

Case 1: Even Number

Enter a number: 6

6 is an Even number.

Case 2: Odd Number

Enter a number: 9

9 is an Odd number.

// Program that calculates the sum of positive numbers out of 10 inputs using the continue statement.

```c
#include <stdio.h>
    int main()
    {
    int num, sum = 0;
    // Loop to get 10 inputs
    for (int i = 1; i <= 10; i++) {
    printf("Enter number %d: ", i);
    scanf("%d", &num);
```

```c
// If number is negative, skip this iteration using continue
if (num < 0) {
continue;
}
// Add positive number to sum
sum += num;
}
// Output the sum of positive numbers
printf("Sum of positive numbers = %d\n", sum);
return 0;
}
```

Output:

Case 1:

Enter number 1: 5

Enter number 2: -3

Enter number 3: 8

Enter number 4: -1

Enter number 5: 12

Enter number 6: -7

Enter number 7: 4

Enter number 8: -2

Enter number 9: 6

Enter number 10: 0

Sum of positive numbers = 35

Explanation: The positive numbers entered are 5, 8, 12, 4, 6, 0, and their sum is 35.

Case 2:

Enter number 1: -2

Enter number 2: -3

Enter number 3: -1

Enter number 4: -4

Enter number 5: -5

Enter number 6: -6
Enter number 7: -7
Enter number 8: -8
Enter number 9: -9
Enter number 10: -10
Sum of positive numbers = 0
Explanation: Since all numbers are negative, the sum is 0.